Behavior and Movement of Adult Summer Steelhead Following Collection and Release, Lower Cowlitz River, Washington, 2012–2013

By Tobias J. Kock, Theresa L. Liedtke, Brian K. Ekstrom, and Dennis W. Rondorf, U.S. Geological Survey; Chris Gleizes and Wolf Dammers, Washington Department of Fish and Wildlife; and Scott Gibson and Jamie Murphy, Tacoma Power

Open-File Report 2013–1116

U.S. Department of the Interior
U.S. Geological Survey

U.S. Department of the Interior
SALLY JEWELL, Secretary

U.S. Geological Survey
Suzette M. Kimball, Acting Director

U.S. Geological Survey, Reston, Virginia: 2013

For more information on the USGS—the Federal source for science about the Earth,
its natural and living resources, natural hazards, and the environment—visit
http://www.usgs.gov or call 1–888–ASK–USGS

For an overview of USGS information products, including maps, imagery, and publications,
visit *http://www.usgs.gov/pubprod*

To order this and other USGS information products, visit *http://store.usgs.gov*

Suggested citation:
Kock, T.J., Liedtke, T.L., Ekstrom, B.K., Rondorf, D.W., Gleizes, C., Dammers, W., Gibson, S., and Murphy, J.,
2013, Behavior and movement of adult summer steelhead following collection and release, lower Cowlitz River,
Washington, 2012–2013: U.S. Geological Survey Open-File Report 2013-1116, 22 p.

Contents

Figures

Tables

Conversion Factors

Inch/Pound to SI

Multiply	By	To obtain
Length		
foot (ft)	0.3048	meter (m)
mile (mi)	1.609	kilometer (km)
Flow rate		
foot per second (ft/s)	0.3048	meter per second (m/s)
cubic foot per second (ft^3/s)	0.02832	cubic meter per second (m^3/s)

SI to Inch/Pound

Multiply	By	To obtain
Length		
centimeter (cm)	0.3937	inch (in.)
millimeter (mm)	0.03937	inch (in.)

Behavior and Movement of Adult Summer Steelhead Following Collection and Release, Lower Cowlitz River, Washington, 2012–2013

By Tobias J. Kock, Theresa L. Liedtke, Brian K. Ekstrom, and Dennis W. Rondorf, U.S. Geological Survey; Chris Gleizes and Wolf Dammers, Washington Department of Fish and Wildlife; and Scott Gibson and Jamie Murphy, Tacoma Power

Executive Summary

Historically, adult summer steelhead *Oncorhynchus mykiss* returning to hatcheries on the lower Cowlitz River were sometimes transported and released in the river (recycled) to provide additional angling opportunity for the popular sport fishery in the basin. However, this practice has not been used in recent years because of concerns associated with interactions between hatchery fish and wild fish. Fishery managers were interested in resuming recycling but lacked information regarding effects of this practice on wild steelhead so we conducted a study during 2012–2013 to: (1) enumerate recycled steelhead that returned to the hatchery or were removed by anglers; and (2) determine if steelhead that were not removed from the river remained in the system where they could interact with wild fish.

During June–August 2012, a total of 549 summer steelhead were captured at the Cowlitz Salmon Hatchery, tagged, and released downstream near the Interstate 5 Bridge. All recycled steelhead were tagged with a white Floy® tag and opercle-punched; 109 (20 percent) of these fish also were radio-tagged. All adult steelhead that return to the hatchery were handled by hatchery staff so recycled steelhead that returned to the hatchery were enumerated daily. A creel survey and voluntary angler reports were used to determine the number of recycled steelhead that were caught by anglers. We established three fixed telemetry monitoring sites on the mainstem Cowlitz River and eight additional sites were deployed on tributaries to the lower Cowlitz River where wild winter steelhead are known to spawn. We also conducted mobile tracking from a boat during October 2012, November 2012, and January 2013 to locate radio-tagged fish.

A total of 10,722 summer steelhead were captured at the Cowlitz Salmon Hatchery in 2012, which was the largest return since 2008. River flows during much of the study period were similar to 2008–2011 average flows, however, high-flow periods in July and November 2012 were nearly twice as high as the 2008–2011 average flows. We determined that 50 percent (273 fish) of the recycled steelhead returned to the hatchery and 18 percent (102 fish) of the recycled steelhead were caught by anglers. Most (243 fish; 89 percent) of the recycled steelhead that returned to the hatchery were recollected during July–August. The average elapsed time from release to recapture at the hatchery was 9 days (d) and 72 percent (182 fish) of the fish returned to the hatchery within 14 d of release. These trends were similar for recycled steelhead that were caught by anglers. Most fish were caught during July–August and the median time from release to capture was 10 d. We determined that 65 percent (70 fish) of the angler-caught fish returned to the hatchery within 14 d of release. River flows appeared to affect both hatchery returns and angler catch. The daily number of recycled steelhead that were recollected at the hatchery were low during periods when river flows were decreasing and high during periods when river flows were increasing. Conversely, daily angler catch of recycled steelhead generally was low when flows were increasing and high when flows were decreasing.

We determined that 32 percent of the recycled steelhead (174 fish) were not removed from the lower Cowlitz River, based on observations from hatchery returns and angler reports, but results from the radio-tagged fish were insightful for understanding what may have happened to these fish. By comparison, we determined that 24 percent of the radio-tagged fish were not known to have been removed from the river. We determined that 12 percent of these fish were actively moving in the lower Cowlitz River during October 2012–January 2013. None of the radio-tagged fish were detected in tributaries during the study period except for a single fish that spent approximately 7 d in the Toutle River during early September. During October 2012–January 2013, 10 percent of the radio-tags from recycled steelhead were detected near popular fishing areas, and 2 percent of the radio-tagged steelhead were never detected during the study period. We suspect that a large proportion of these fish may have been harvested and not reported, or died.

Detection patterns of radio-tagged steelhead showed that most fish (82 percent) moved upstream from the release site and were detected at the Trout Hatchery and the Barrier Dam sites. The median time from release to detection at these sites was 3.7 d and many of these fish made multiple trips between the two sites. Nearly one-third (29 percent) of the recycled steelhead that were detected at the Trout Hatchery and the Barrier Dam made at least two trips between the sites and some fish made as many as six trips. Radio-tagged fish that remained in the lower Cowlitz River during the spawning period (December 2012–January 2013) were observed in the river reach between the mouth of Ostrander Creek (river mile 10) and the Trout Hatchery (river mile 44).

During this study, we collected data on opercle punch regrowth rates to understand the temporal effectiveness of this marking technique. We took opercle measurements for a total of 190 fish during the study. Fresh opercle punches were measured for 63 fish at the time of marking, and the remaining 127 fish were measured when fish returned to the hatchery. We determined that opercle punches remained open for about 30 d. The holes appeared to regrow slowly in the first 20 d after marking, but regrowth accelerated during the 20–30 d post-marking period. After 30 d, all opercle punches that we observed had completely closed due to tissue regrowth.

Our study showed that a large proportion (68 percent) of the recycled steelhead were removed from the lower Cowlitz River. These fish primarily entered the hatchery or were caught by anglers within 14 d of release, which suggests that they present minimal risk to wild fish in the system. However, the remaining fish (32 percent) could not be accounted for, which may complicate fisheries management decisions associated with recycling summer steelhead. Findings from the radiotelemetry study suggest that unreported harvest or mortality could explain a large proportion of those fish that were not reported as having been removed from the river. Furthermore, intensive monitoring of the key spawning tributaries failed to detect a single fish during the spawning period. These findings were supported by observations from weir traps operated by the Washington Department of Fish and Wildlife. Our findings indicate that additional research may be warranted to further examine the effects of recycling hatchery summer steelhead in the lower Cowlitz River.

Introduction

The management of many Pacific salmon *Oncorhynchus* spp. populations is complicated by the conflicting need to maintain production of hatchery-produced (hereafter hatchery) fish while also protecting or rebuilding stocks of naturally produced (hereafter wild) fish. Hatchery salmon production is necessary to support harvest in many rivers throughout the Pacific Northwest, western Canada, and Alaska because many of the wild salmon populations in these areas have declined to levels where extinction is possible. However, efforts to maintain hatchery salmon populations and rebuild wild salmon populations often conflict. Hatchery salmon have been shown to influence wild salmon through predation, competition for space and resources, and by lowering the fitness of wild populations where interbreeding occurs (Hindar and others, 1991; Waples, 1991; Berejikian and others, 1996; Noakes and others, 2000; Naman and Sharpe, 2012; Rand and others, 2012). Given these concerns, contemporary fisheries management strategies for hatchery salmon typically try to reduce impacts that could jeopardize wild salmon in a given system.

Steelhead *Oncorhynchus mykiss* are an important resource in the Cowlitz River, a primary tributary to the lower Columbia River, in southwestern Washington State. The Cowlitz River supports three distinct steelhead populations including wild winter, hatchery winter, and hatchery summer stocks. Adult wild and hatchery winter steelhead return to the system during December–April and spawn during March–May. Adult hatchery summer steelhead return during May–October and spawn primarily during December–January. Wild winter steelhead in the Cowlitz River are currently listed as threatened under the U.S. Endangered Species Act (Lower Columbia River evolutionary significant unit [ESU]; National Marine Fisheries Service, 2011), whereas adult hatchery (winter and summer stocks) steelhead support popular sport fisheries in the system.

Historically, some of the summer steelhead that returned to the hatchery during the early portion of the run (June–July) were collected and transported downstream to a release site on the lower Cowlitz River. This strategy was referred to as "recycling" and supplemented the number of adult hatchery steelhead in the system, thereby increasing angling opportunity. During recent years, steelhead recycling has not occurred because of the perceived risks to wild fish. Definitive studies have not been conducted on the lower Cowlitz River to quantify recycled hatchery steelhead that remained in the system, or to determine if these fish interacted with wild fish. This type of evaluation was of interest to the Washington Department of Fish and Wildlife (WDFW) because the recycling program could benefit anglers in the lower Cowlitz River if research showed that recycled summer steelhead were not affecting wild winter steelhead.

We conducted an evaluation during 2012–2013 to determine the fate of recycled summer steelhead in the lower Cowlitz River. Recycling adult summer steelhead has two primary consequences of interest: (1) increased angler opportunity and harvest if recycled steelhead are caught by anglers; and (2) increased risk to wild winter steelhead populations if recycled fish are not caught by anglers, remain in the system, and compete against, or spawn with wild winter steelhead. Given these potential consequences, the goals of this study were to monitor the behavior and movement of recycled steelhead and to quantify the fish that returned to the hatchery fish trap, were caught by anglers, or remained in the Cowlitz River (or a tributary of the Cowlitz River) where they could potentially interact with wild steelhead.

Methods

Fish Tagging and Release

A total of 549 adult summer steelhead were captured at the Cowlitz Salmon Hatchery (river mile [rm] 51; fig. 1), tagged, and then transported downstream and released into the lower Cowlitz River (rm 30). Each fish was tagged with a white Floy® tag (Model FD-68BC; Floy® Tag, Inc., Seattle, Washington) near the dorsal fin, and a single 6-mm diameter hole was created in the operculum (hereafter opercle punch) using a hand punch (fig. 2). We also tagged 109 (20 percent) of these fish with a radio transmitter (Model Pisces; Sigma Eight Inc., Newmarket, Ontario) to monitor behavior and movement patterns during the study. A total of 10 tagging and release events were conducted during June–August 2012 (table 1). On each tagging date, adult summer steelhead were collected by hatchery staff as part of the daily collection process. Groups of fish (approximately 20 fish per group) were crowded into a large basket and anesthetized using the hatchery's electroanesthesia system. Each batch of fish was then sorted and summer steelhead were selected for tagging if they had not previously been tagged. Each fish was measured for fork length to the nearest centimeter, visually categorized as male or female, and then Floy® tagged and opercle punched. Fish that received radio transmitters also were tagged during this time. All tagged fish were then placed into a hatchery holding tank where they were held for approximately 24 h. On each release date, tagged fish were loaded onto large fish-hauling trucks, transported downstream, and released at the Interstate 5 boat ramp (fig. 1).

Opercle punches are popular fish marking techniques because they are inexpensive and can be easily identified when fish are handled and visually examined. However, they are not a permanent marking technique because the hole can eventually close because of tissue regrowth. Although opercle punches commonly are used, there was little information regarding regrowth rates; so we collected data during this study to better understand the temporal effectiveness of the technique. We used a digital electronic caliper to measure the inside diameter of a subset of opercle punches when fish were tagged or re-collected at the hatchery. These measurements were paired with Floy® tag identification numbers so that we could determine the elapsed time between tagging of the fish and re-collection when the opercle punches were measured.

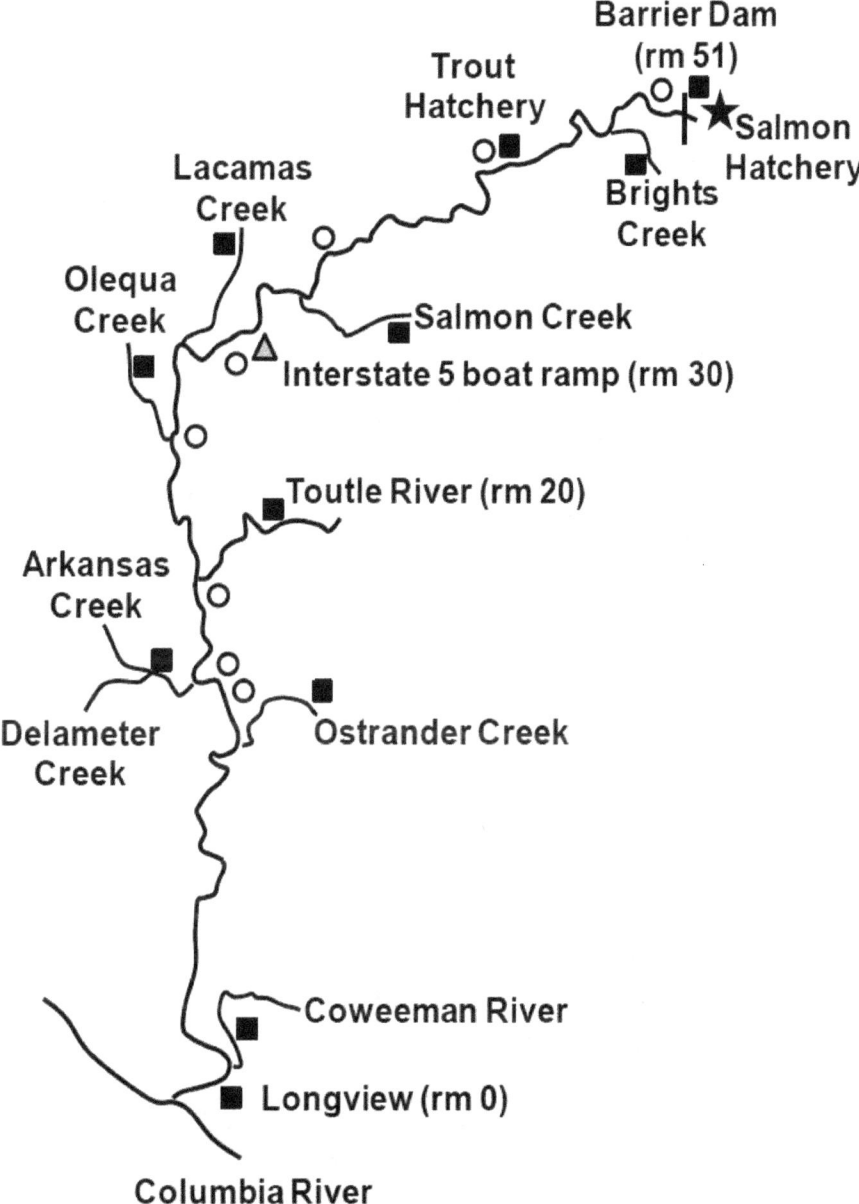

Figure 1. Schematic of the lower Cowlitz River and tributaries, Washington, that were monitored for the presence of radio-tagged adult steelhead during an evaluation in 2012. The locations of fixed radiotelemetry monitoring sites (squares), creel survey sites (circles), and the fish release site (triangle) are shown.

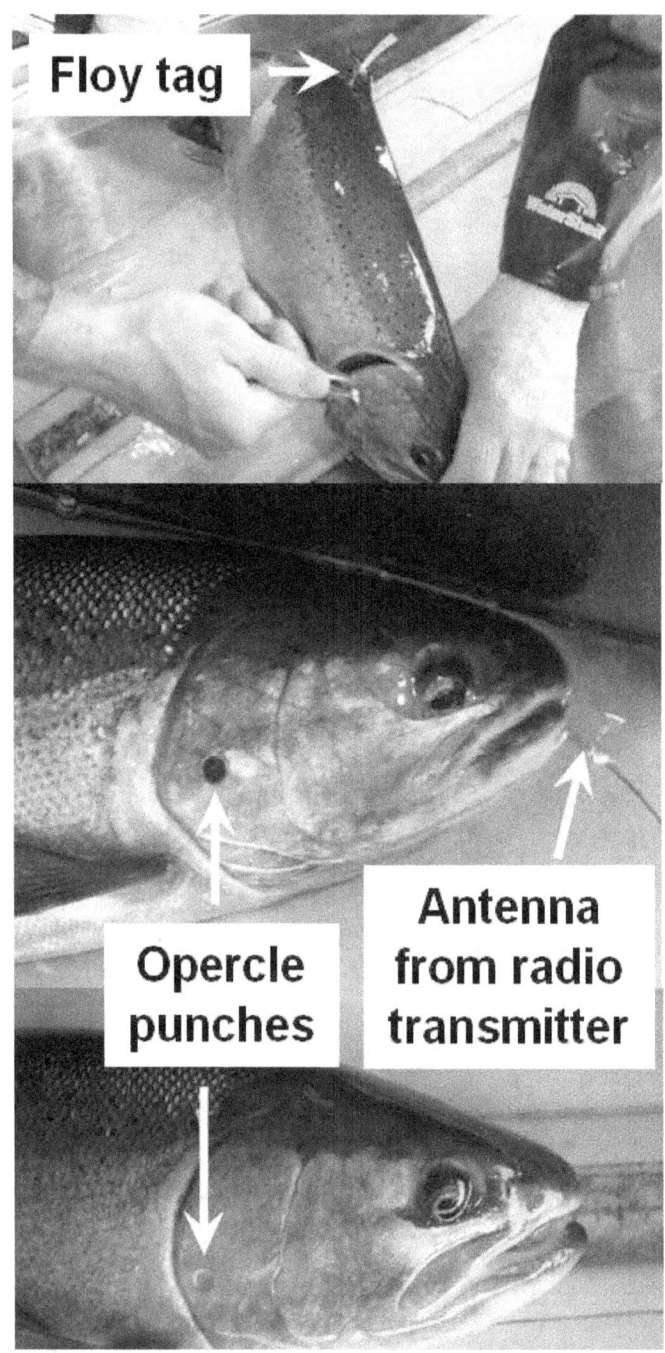

Figure 2. Photographs showing a Floy®-tagged steelhead that was being opercle punched (top); a fresh opercle punch and a radio transmitter antenna exiting the fish mouth (transmitter was located inside the fish and is not visible) (middle); and an opercle punch that had closed from tissue re-growth (bottom). Photographs taken by Tobias J. Kock, U.S. Geological Survey, July 23, 2012.

Table 1. Tagging dates and numbers of adult hatchery steelhead that were marked for an evaluation on the lower Cowlitz River, Washington, 2012.

Tagging date	Number of fish that were radio-tagged, Floy®-tagged, and opercle punched	Number of fish that were Floy® tagged and opercle punched	Total number of fish marked and released
June 18	12	25	37
June 25	1	30	31
July 2	16	40	56
July 9	5	50	55
July 16	15	65	80
July 23	7	70	77
July 30	17	60	77
August 6	3	50	53
August 13	25	30	55
August 20	8	20	28
Totals	109	440	549

Fish Monitoring

We collected data on recycled steelhead using three primary approaches during 2012: (1) monitoring at the hatchery to quantify recycled steelhead that were recollected; (2) conducting a creel survey and collecting voluntary angler reports to estimate the number of recycled steelhead that were caught by anglers; and (3) monitoring movements of radio-tagged fish through fixed monitoring sites (hereafter fixed sites) and mobile tracking.

The fish trap at the Cowlitz Salmon Hatchery was operated 5 days per week (Monday–Friday) and hatchery personnel examined summer steelhead that were captured in the trap during June–December 2012 to identify recycled fish. Recycled steelhead were identified by the presence of at least one of the three tags or marks (that is, white Floy® tag, opercle punch, or radio transmitter) used during our study. Floy® tags and radio transmitters can be shed and opercle punches can close from tissue regrowth (fig. 2), and in some cases, fish were identified based only on the presence of a closed opercle punch. When recycled steelhead were encountered at the hatchery, the Floy®-tag and radio-tag (when present) were removed and the identification numbers and recapture date were recorded. If a steelhead returned without a Floy® tag or radio transmitter then only the recapture date was recorded. Recycled steelhead that were encountered in the fish trap were retained at the Cowlitz Salmon Hatchery and not re-released into the lower Cowlitz River.

A creel survey and voluntary angler reporting were used to quantify recycled steelhead that were captured and retained in the fishery during the study period. The creel survey was conducted during June–December 2012. Angling is popular throughout the lower Cowlitz River so we attempted to visit multiple sites on each survey date to maximize the number of anglers interviewed and to account for spatial differences in harvest. Creel surveys targeted popular fishing locations in the lower Cowlitz River including the Barrier Dam (rm 51), Trout Hatchery (rm 44), Mission Bar (rm 37), the Interstate 5 boat ramp (rm 30), Olequa Creek (rm 25), the mouth of the Toutle River (rm 20), the town of Castle Rock (rm 17), and Camelot (rm 15; fig. 1). Anglers were interviewed to determine the number of hours fished and the number of fish that were caught. Adult steelhead that were retained by anglers were enumerated and recycled steelhead were identified and enumerated using criteria previously described. We also distributed information about the study to local fishing shops, on regional fishing websites, and at popular boat ramps and fishing locations in the system so that anglers could voluntarily report information when recycled steelhead were caught.

We established three fixed radiotelemetry sites on the mainstem lower Cowlitz River and eight fixed sites on tributaries to the lower Cowlitz River to monitor behavior and movement patterns of radio-tagged steelhead during the study. Mainstem fixed sites were located at the Barrier Dam, the Trout Hatchery and near the mouth of the Cowlitz River (rm 1; fig. 1). Tributary fixed sites were established on Brights Creek, Salmon Creek, Lacamas Creek, Olequa Creek, the Toutle River, at the confluence of Arkansas and Delameter Creeks, Ostrander Creek, and the Coweeman River (fig. 1). Fixed sites continuously monitored for the presence of tagged fish from June 2012 to January 2013. To supplement fixed site detections, we conducted three mobile tracking surveys from a boat on the mainstem Cowlitz River. Mobile tracking surveys were conducted on October 9, 2012, November 19, 2012, and January 9, 2013. The first and last mobile tracking surveys included the area between the Barrier Dam boat launch (rm 51) and the town of Longview (rm 0. The second mobile tracking survey had limited scope because of hazardous weather conditions and included the area between the Barrier Dam boat launch and the mouth of the Toutle River (rm 20).

Results

Run Size, Run Timing, and River Flows

A total of 10,722 summer steelhead were captured at the hatchery during April–December 2012, which is the highest total since 2008. During 2008–2011, annual collection of adult summer steelhead averaged 6,989 fish and ranged from a low of 5,150 fish in 2009 to a high of 8,908 fish in 2010. The pattern of arrival timing for summer steelhead at the hatchery during 2012 was similar to trends observed during 2008–2011 (fig. 3). Fish began returning to the hatchery in mid-April and continued to be collected through December. Most fish (91 percent) were collected during June–September (fig. 3). River flows are an important factor that can affect migration behavior of adult fish, hatchery returns, angler effort, and angler success. We examined river flows during 2012 and compared them to river flows during 2008–2011 to determine if flow conditions were typical during the study period. Average (daily mean) river flows in 2008–2011 were plotted against 2012 flows (fig. 4) to visually assess the relationship during these periods. To determine how flows differed during these periods, we calculated a ratio that compared 2012 flows to 2008–2011 flows. A daily flow ratio statistic was calculated for each date from June to November by dividing the daily flow from 2012 by the average daily flow from 2008 to 2011. For example, on July 17, 2012, flow in the lower Cowlitz River was 10,500 ft^3/s and the 2008–2011 average flow on this date was 5,430 ft^3/s. The ratio was calculated as 10,500/5,430=1.9, which indicates that flows on July 17, 2012 were 1.9 times higher than the 2008–2011 average flow. This ratio was plotted across the study period (fig. 4) to describe how 2012 flows varied with respect to 2008–2011 flows. This graph shows that flows were near normal (that is, ratio of 1.0) during much of the study period except during July and November when 2012 flows frequently were 1.5–2.0 times higher than normal.

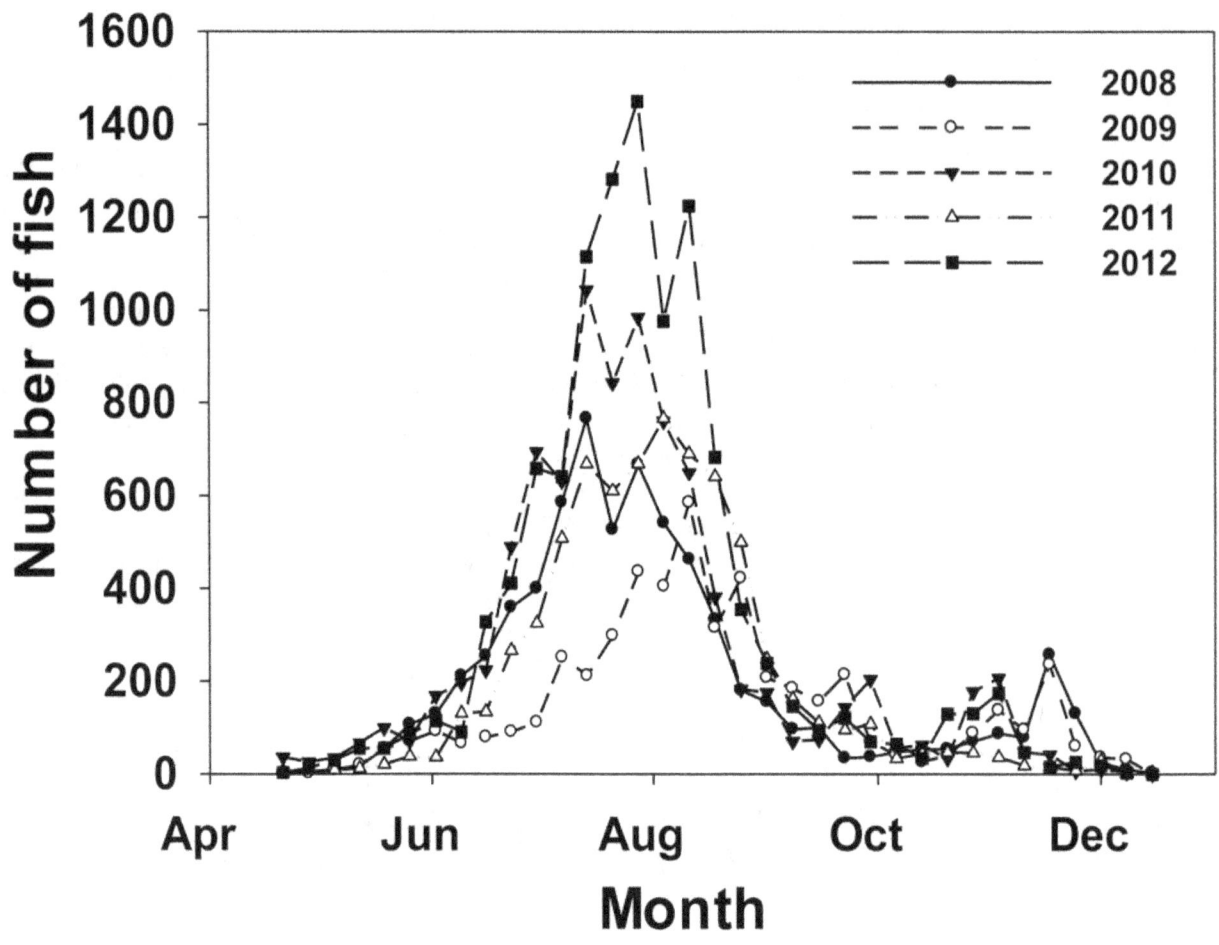

Figure 3. Arrival timing of adult summer steelhead at the Cowlitz Salmon Hatchery, Washington, 2008–2012.

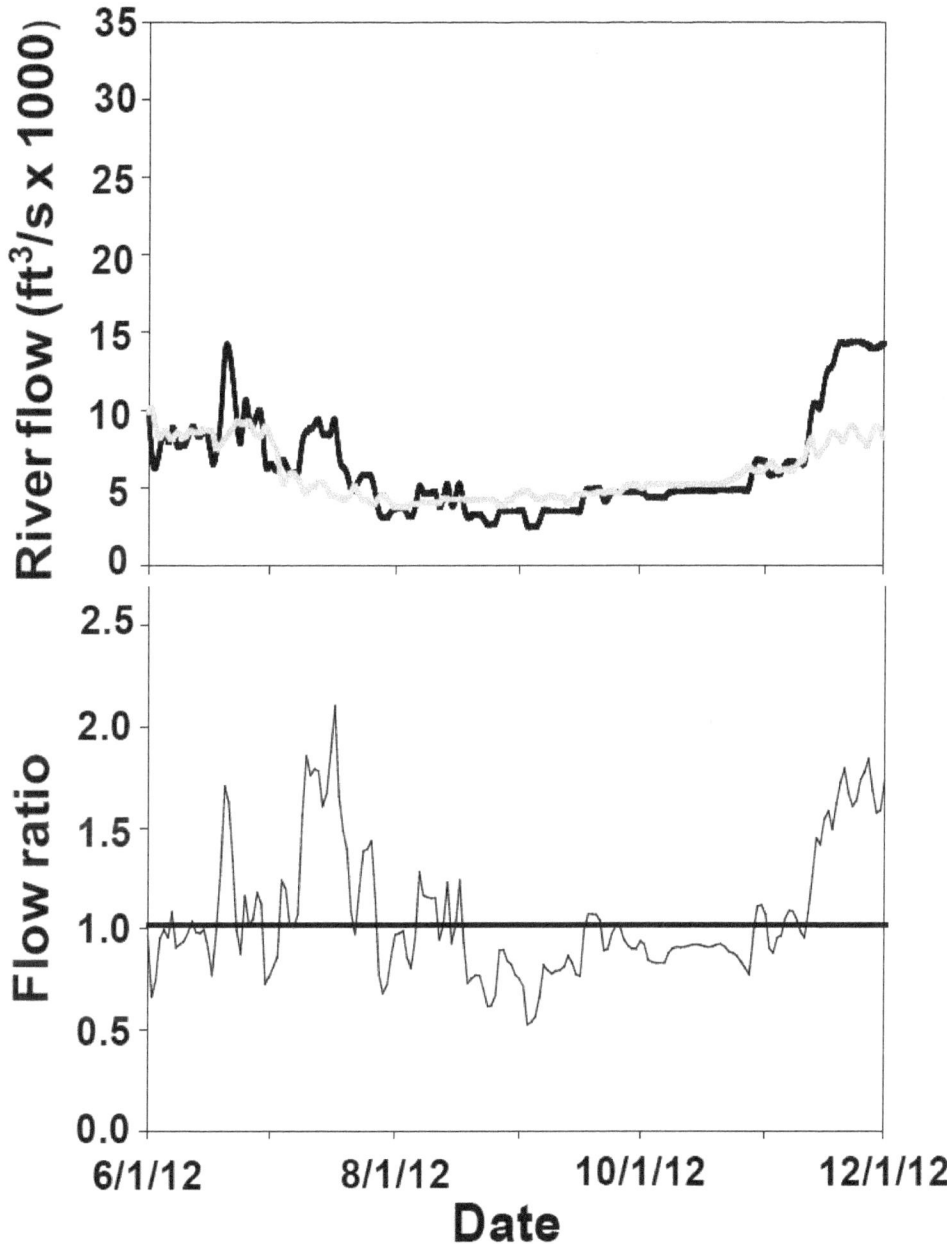

Figure 4. Graphs showing daily river flows (thousand cubic feet per sec [k ft³/s]; top) measured near Mayfield Dam (USGS streamgage No. 14238000) during June–December 2012 (black line) and average river flows during the same period from 2008 to 2011 (gray line); the relationship between 2012 and average 2008–2011 flows (bottom). Flow ratio of 1.0 indicates that 2012 flows were identical to 2008–2011 flows. Flow ratios less than 1.0 indicate that 2012 flows were lower than 2008–2011 flows and flow ratios greater than 1.0 indicate that 2012 flows were higher than 2008–2011 flows.

Hatchery Returns

One-half of the steelhead that were recycled during the study eventually returned to the hatchery and most of the returning fish spent 2 weeks or less in the river after being transported. A total of 549 steelhead were recycled during the study and 273 (50 percent; table 2) of these fish were re-collected at the hatchery. Some of the steelhead that returned to the hatchery did not retain the Floy® tag (15 fish; 6 percent) or the recapture date was not recorded (6 fish; 2 percent) so we could not determine residence time (recapture date–release date) in the lower Cowlitz River of these fish. However, most of the steelhead that returned to the hatchery did retain their tags and had valid return date data (252 fish; 92 percent). The median residence time in the lower Cowlitz River for fish that returned to the hatchery was 9 d (days) (range = 3–105 d) and most fish (182 fish; 72 percent) returned to the hatchery within 14 d of release. Most recycled steelhead returned to the hatchery during July and August (fig. 5) but some fish returned through mid-October.

Table 2. Summary of the fate of recycled steelhead that were released for a study on the Cowlitz River, Washington, 2012.

[Data are shown for all fish tagged during the study (including radio-tagged fish) and radio-tagged fish only]

Fate	All fish	Radio-tagged fish
	Number of fish	Number of fish
Hatchery return	273 (50 percent)	52 (48 percent)
Angler caught	102 (18 percent)	30 (28 percent)
Cowlitz River		13 (12 percent)
Mortality or regurgitated transmitter		11 (10 percent)
Not detected		3 (2 percent)
Unknown	174 (32 percent)	0
Total	549	109

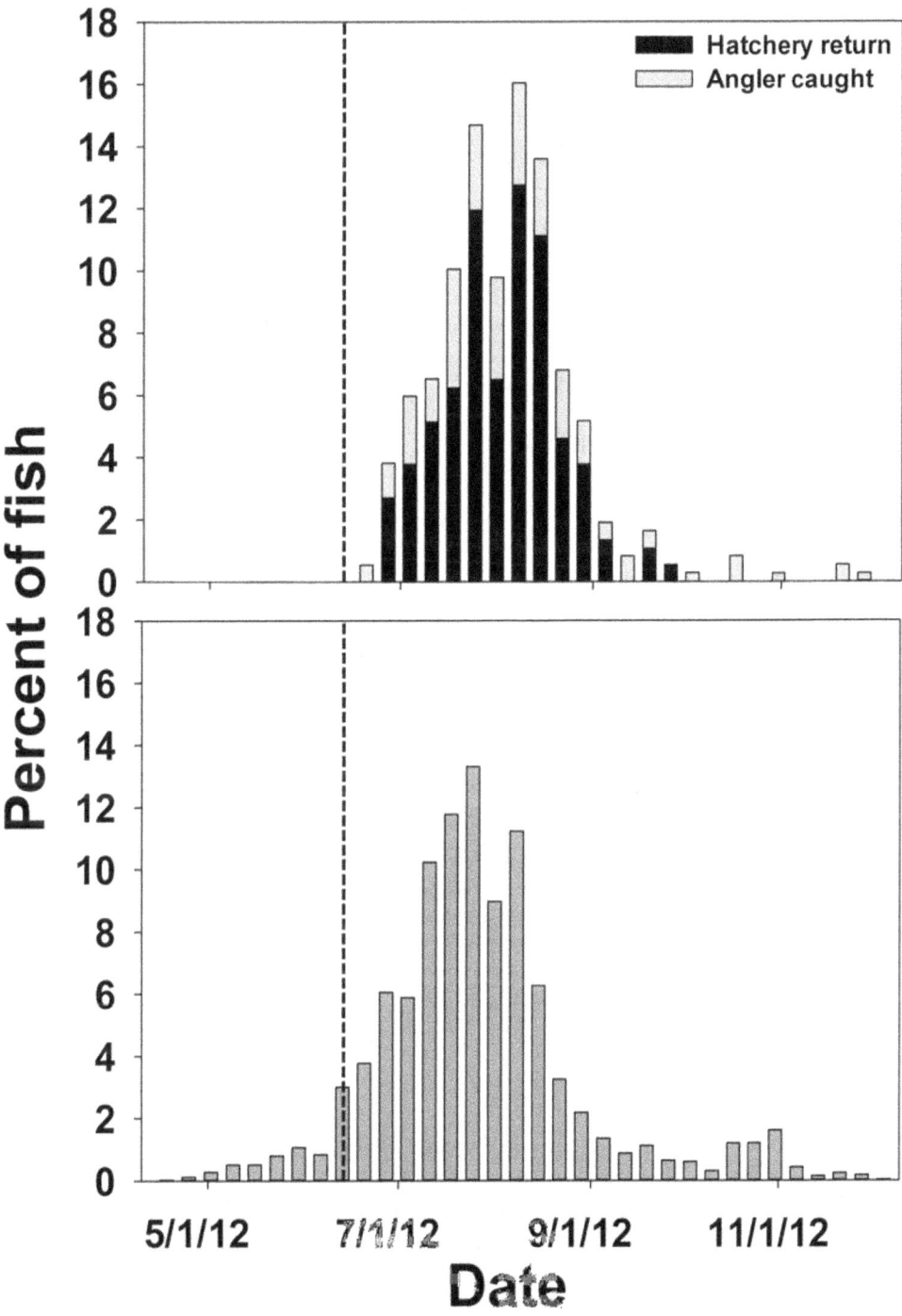

Figure 5. Graphs showing percentage of recycled steelhead that returned to the hatchery or were caught by anglers (top) and run timing for summer steelhead in the Cowlitz River based on the number of fish that were collected at the Cowlitz Salmon Hatchery (bottom), lower Cowlitz River, Washington. Vertical dashed line denotes when recycling began.

Angler Harvest

Anglers reported harvesting 102 (18 percent; table 2) recycled steelhead during the study period. Voluntary angler reporting accounted for the majority (90 fish; 88 percent) of the harvest data but some recycled steelhead were recorded in the creel survey (12 fish; 12 percent). During the creel survey, 2,947 anglers were interviewed and these anglers harvested a total of 594 summer steelhead. Recycled steelhead composed 2 percent of the catch during this period. Trends in angler harvest were similar to those observed for hatchery returns because most fish were caught during July–August (fig. 5). However, anglers continued to catch low numbers of recycled steelhead through November (fig. 5). The median residence time in the lower Cowlitz River for fish harvested by anglers was 10 d (range = 1–140 d) and most of the fish (70 fish; 65 percent) were caught within 14 d of release.

Effect of Release Timing and River Flow on Fate of Recycled Steelhead

Steelhead were assigned to one of three fates (returned to the hatchery, harvested by anglers, not removed from the river) for each release group to determine if there were temporal trends in the fates of recycled steelhead (fig. 6). For most release groups, the largest percentage of fish returned to the hatchery and the smallest percentage of fish were caught by anglers (fig. 6). These trends were consistent throughout the study period (fig. 6).

We plotted the daily number of steelhead that returned to the hatchery or were harvested by anglers against daily river flows from mid-June through August, when most fish were removed from the river, to determine if there were any apparent trends (fig. 7). The number of fish that returned to the hatchery each day generally increased during this period (fig. 7). Flow also appeared to affect hatchery returns; flows generally were decreasing on days when no fish returned to the hatchery and generally were increasing on the highest collection days (fig. 7). Conversely, there was no apparent temporal trend in angler harvest (fig. 7). River flows appeared to affect angler harvest although the relationship between these factors was opposite of that which was observed between river flows and hatchery returns; anglers generally caught more fish during days when flows were decreasing and catch numbers were low on days when river flows were increasing (fig. 7).

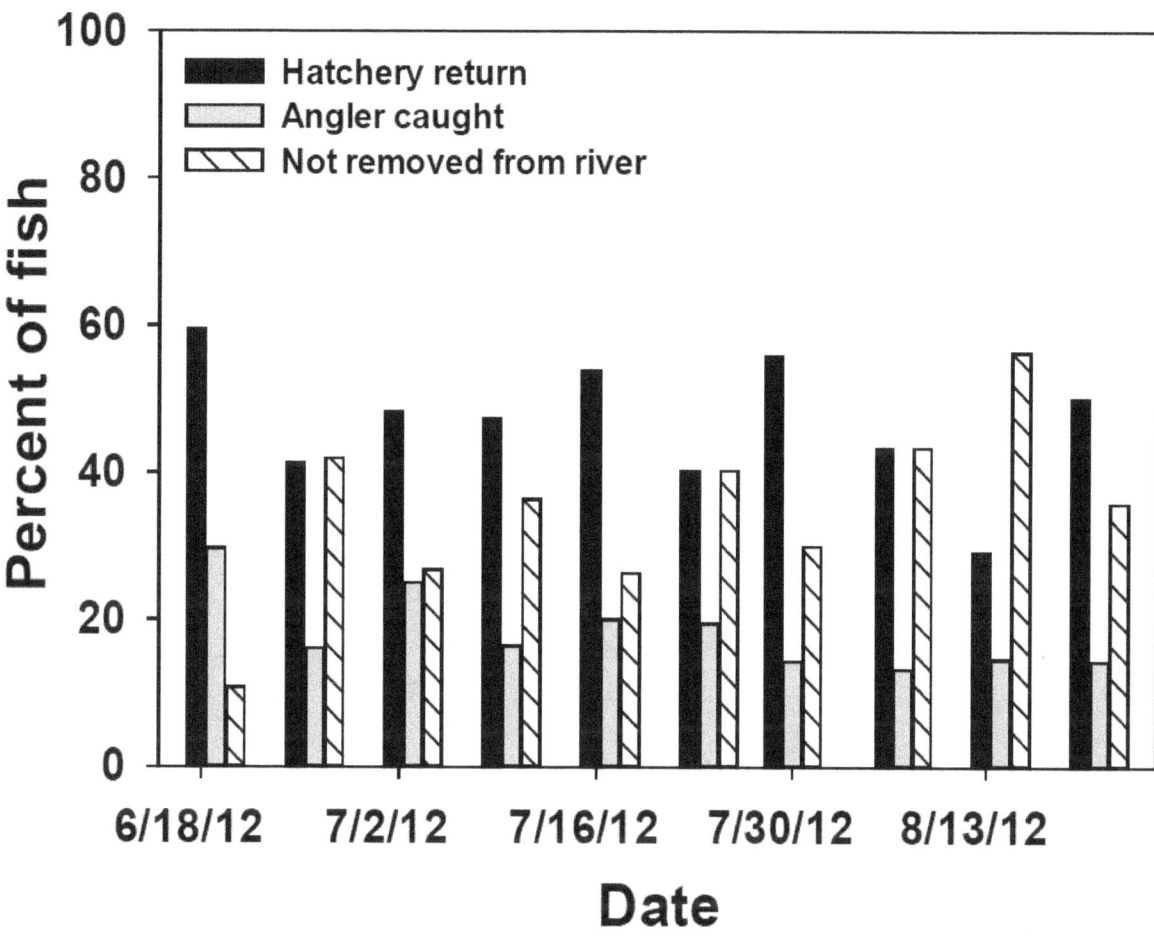

Figure 6. Graph showing percent of recycled steelhead from each release group that returned to the hatchery, were caught by anglers, or were not known to be removed from the lower Cowlitz River, Washington, 2012.

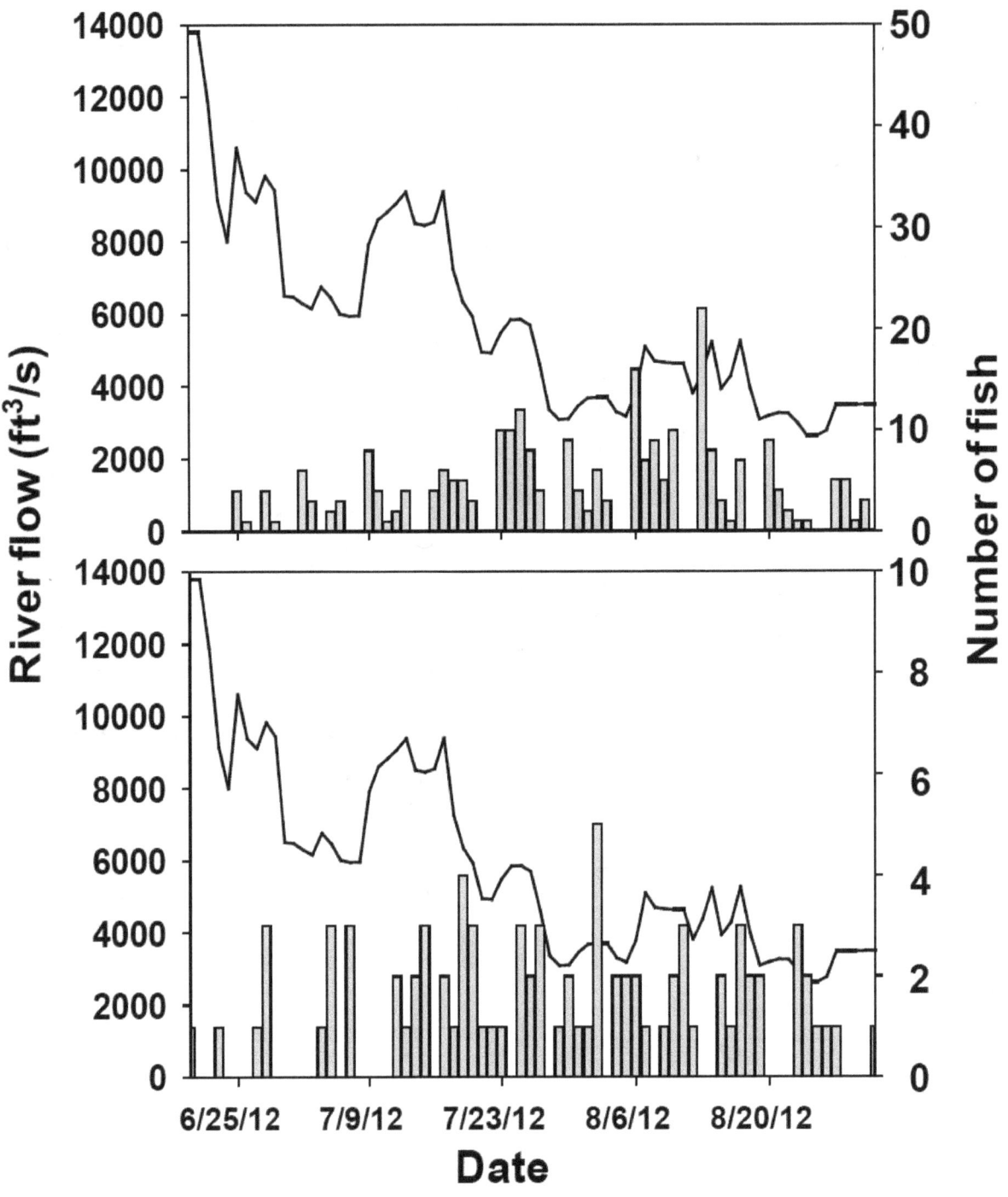

Figure 7. Graphs showing number of fish that returned to the hatchery (top graph) or were caught by anglers (bottom graph) each day (gray bars) and daily river flows (black line) during a study on the lower Cowlitz River , Washington, 2012. Data are presented from mid-June through August when most fish returned to the hatchery or were caught by anglers.

Radiotelemetry

Radio-tagged fish provided valuable information because we were able to determine the fates of fish that were not removed from the river, monitor tributaries for the presence of tagged fish, and describe behavior patterns of fish prior to entering the hatchery or being caught by anglers. Most radio-tagged fish returned to the hatchery (50 fish; 48 percent) or were caught by anglers (30 fish; 28 percent; table 2). The remaining radio-tagged fish (27 fish; 24 percent) were not known to have been removed from the river so we examined detection histories of these fish to determine their fate. Detection histories from fixed sites and mobile tracking events were used to determine if individual fish were moving within the lower Cowlitz River during October 2012–January 2013, which would indicate that a given fish was alive. We detected 13 (12 percent) radio-tagged fish moving within the lower Cowlitz River during this period. Additionally, 11 (10 percent) radio-tagged fish were detected in the lower Cowlitz River that did not exhibit movement during October 2012–January 2013. This detection pattern indicated that the fish had died, or had regurgitated the transmitter. Ten (91 percent) of these tags were located near popular angling areas including the Barrier Dam (1 fish), Trout Hatchery (4 fish), Mission Bar (2 fish), town of Toledo (2 fish), and the Interstate 5 boat launch (1 fish), which could indicate that tags were removed from fish or that fish died after being hooked. The remaining fish (3 fish; 2 percent) were never detected during the study (table 2).

Detection records show that most radio-tagged fish moved upstream from the release site and were detected in the river reach between the Barrier Dam and the Trout Hatchery during June–October. In total, 89 of the radio-tagged fish (82 percent) moved upstream following release and were detected at the Trout Hatchery or Barrier Dam, or both. The median elapsed time from release to first detection at these sites was 3.7 d (range = 0.8–99.1 d). Many radio-tagged fish made repeated trips between the Trout Hatchery and the Barrier Dam. A single trip consisted of moving one time between the two sites. For example, fish that moved upstream from the Trout Hatchery to the Barrier Dam and then back downstream to the Trout Hatchery made two trips. We determined that 32 radio-tagged fish (29 percent) made at least two trips between the two sites and some fish made up to six trips (fig. 8).

Radio-tagged steelhead moved downstream as the spawning period approached and were detected in the river reach between the Trout Hatchery and the mouth of Ostrander Creek. The last detection of any radio-tagged fish at the Barrier Dam occurred on November 8. Three radio-tagged fish were detected at the mouth of the Cowlitz River but these fish remained in the system and were later detected upstream during mobile tracking. During November 2012–January 2013, all radio-tagged fish were detected either at the Trout Hatchery site, or in the river reach between the Trout Hatchery and the mouth of Ostrander Creek (by mobile tracking).

We only detected one radio-tagged fish (<1 percent) on any of the tributary monitoring sites and this detection occurred prior to the spawning period. That fish was released on August 14 and was subsequently detected at the Trout Hatchery and Barrier Dam sites multiple times during August 16–26. The fish then entered the Toutle River on August 30 and was later detected on September 7 when it exited the Toutle River and returned to the lower Cowlitz River. The fish was detected in the lower Cowlitz River near the mouth of Ostrander Creek during the October 2012 and January 2013 mobile tracking events.

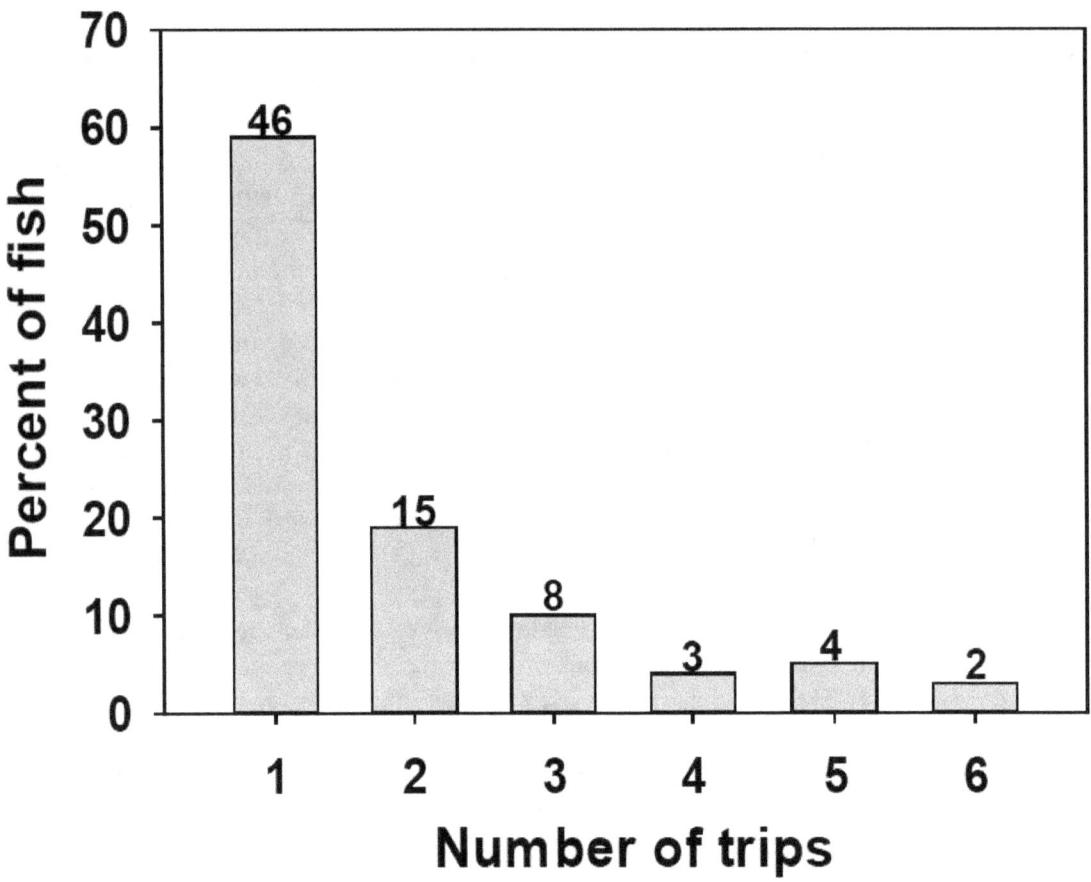

Figure 8. Graph showing percentage of radio-tagged fish observed making trips between the Trout Hatchery and the Barrier Dam during a study on the lower Cowlitz River, Washington, 2012. Numbers above bars are the number of fish in each group.

Temporal Effectiveness of Opercle Punches

We measured the diameter of a total of 190 opercle punches during the study period and determined that the opercle punches remained open for about 30 d (fig. 9). Opercle punch measurements were taken at the time of tagging (63 fish) and when fish returned to the hatchery (127 fish). The diameter of the opercle hole was plotted against the elapsed time since tagging (fig. 9).Opercle regrowth generally was slow during the first 20 d following tagging, but the hole closed quickly between 20 and 30 d after tagging. All steelhead that returned to the hatchery less than 30 d after tagging had opercle punches that had completely closed.

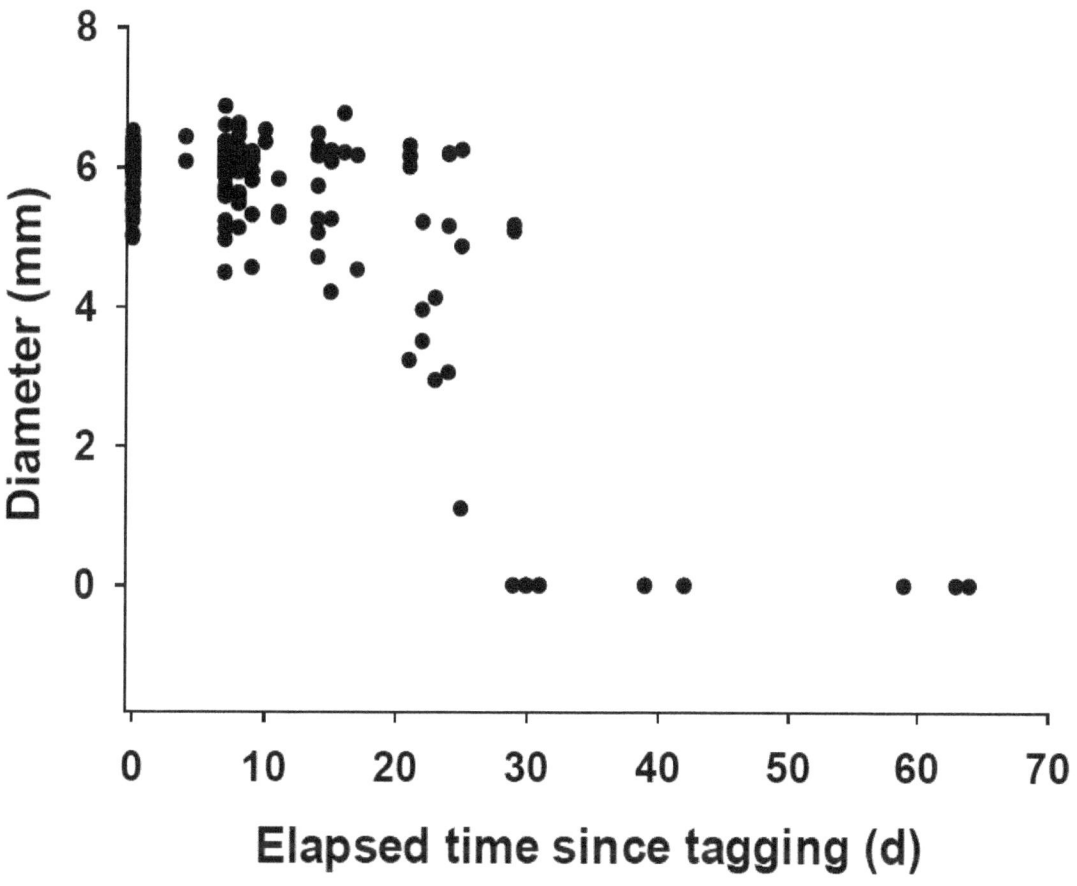

Figure 9. Graph showing relationship between the inside diameter of opercle punches of adult steelhead and the elapsed time in days (d) since tagging for a study on the Cowlitz River, Washington, 2012.

Discussion

Our study showed that a substantial number of recycled steelhead were removed from the Cowlitz River shortly after they were released. We determined that 68 percent of the recycled fish returned to the hatchery or were caught by anglers. Nearly one-half of the recycled steelhead (252 fish; 46 percent) were removed from the river within 14 d of release. Our results demonstrated that recycling summer steelhead was effective at increasing angling opportunities in the system. Anglers harvested a minimum of 18 percent of the fish that were recycled during the study and results from the creel survey showed that 2 percent of the catch during June–December consisted of recycled steelhead. However, approximately one-third (32 percent) of the recycled steelhead were not reported as having been removed from the river.

Results from radio-tagged fish suggest that unreported harvest or mortality could partially explain why some recycled steelhead were not reported as having been removed from the river. We determined that 24 percent of the radio-tagged steelhead did not return to the hatchery or were not caught by anglers. However, only 12 percent of the recycled steelhead were detected in the lower Cowlitz River during the spawning period and no radio-tagged fish were detected in known spawning tributaries during November 2012–January 2013. The remaining radio-tagged fish were either not detected (2 percent) or were determined to have regurgitated a transmitter or died (10 percent), based on continued detections at a single location over a long period of time. We suspect that many of these fish were either harvested and not reported, or the transmitters were removed after a given fish was caught and either released or harvested. Mobile tracking events conducted prior to, and during, the spawning period provided continuous coverage throughout the lower 44 river miles in the lower Cowlitz River. During these mobile tracking events, 91 percent of the fish (10 of 11) that were determined to have died or regurgitated their transmitter were located in close proximity to popular boat ramps and fishing locations (that is, Barrier Dam, Trout Hatchery, Mission Bar, Toledo, and Interstate 5 bridge) in the river. This observation would suggest that anglers contributed to this distribution because we would expect these transmitters to be more randomly distributed throughout the system if mortality or transmitter regurgitation was occurring through random chance. Given these findings, results from the radio-tagged fish suggest that only 12 percent of the recycled steelhead remained in the Cowlitz River during the spawning period. These results illustrate the value of using active transmitters within a fish marking study because we were able to collect data on fish that were not removed from the river, which allowed us to better estimate the percentage of recycled steelhead that remained in the river.

Movement data from radio-tagged fish showed that most recycled steelhead moved quickly upstream following release and were primarily located at, or upstream of, the Trout Hatchery during June–October, then moved downstream and were located between the mouth of Ostrander Creek and the Trout Hatchery during November 2012–January 2013. Most of the recycled steelhead (82 percent) moved upstream and were detected at the Trout Hatchery or the Barrier Dam, or both, shortly after release, and the average elapsed time from release to detection in this reach was less than 4 d. Tagged fish that did not enter the hatchery or were not caught by anglers in this reach tended to move back and forth between the two sites. Nearly one-third (32 percent) of the radio-tagged fish that were detected in this reach made at least two trips between the sites and some fish made as many as six trips each. This behavior diminished over time, however, as tagged fish moved downstream when the spawning period approached. No radio-tagged fish were detected at the Barrier Dam after early November. Three radio-tagged fish were detected at the mouth of the Cowlitz River but these fish remained in the system and were later detected upstream. All radio-tagged fish that were known to be alive during November 2012–January 2013 were detected between the mouth of Ostrander Creek and the Trout Hatchery.

We focused monitoring efforts of radio-tagged fish on known spawning tributaries in the lower Cowlitz River because of concerns that recycled steelhead would interact, and potentially spawn, with wild steelhead in these areas, but findings from this study and others suggest that this did not occur. Most of our fixed sites were located on tributaries to the lower Cowlitz River and these sites only detected one fish during the entire study period. The tagged fish briefly entered the Toutle River before returning to the Cowlitz River. None of the radio-tagged steelhead were detected in the tributaries during the spawning period, which suggests that recycled steelhead did not use these areas to spawn. This observation was supported by findings from weir traps operated by WDFW on lower Cowlitz River tributaries. Weir traps were located on Salmon, Olequa, and Delameter Creeks, and hatchery summer steelhead have not been collected in these traps, although wild and hatchery winter steelhead have been captured there (Washington Department of Fish and Wildlife, unpub. data, 2012). Based on these findings, summer steelhead apparently are not using, or spawning in, lower Cowlitz River tributaries. Given these observations and the documented use of the mainstem Cowlitz River by recycled steelhead during November 2012–January 2013, future evaluations should be considered that focus more intensely on summer steelhead behavior patterns between the Trout Hatchery and Ostrander Creek. Increased monitoring in this reach may provide useful information regarding behavior patterns during the spawning period and also could be insightful for estimating unreported harvest of recycled fish.

Abnormally high flows occurred during early July and November–December 2012 and these are important periods for summer steelhead in the Cowlitz River so results from this study may have been affected. Hatchery returns and angler catch were affected by river flows. Hatchery returns increased and angler catch decreased during periods of increasing river flow and these trends were reversed when river flows were decreasing. Hatchery returns and angler harvest of summer steelhead typically peaks during July so the abnormally high flows measured during July could have influenced findings of the study. High July flows during 2012 may have resulted in higher than normal hatchery returns and lower than normal angler catch, when compared with normal flow periods. Hatchery summer steelhead in the Cowlitz River typically spawn during December so the higher than normal November–December flows could have influenced the fish distribution during this time. Radio-tagged fish were all located between the Trout Hatchery and the mouth of Ostrander Creek and it is possible that these fish were responding to the high flows, rather than targeting a specific river reach.

Finally, we were able to collect data on the retention time of opercle punches and our results suggest that this marking technique may be effective for about 30 d under the conditions we observed. We found that regrowth rates were relatively slow within about 21 d of the marking event. However, every fish that was recovered at the hatchery more than 30 d after tagging had opercle punches that were completely closed. These marks remained visible after tissue regrowth, but it is unclear how long this would remain true. Our results suggest that opercle punches should be considered short-term marking techniques until additional studies have been conducted to evaluate their effectiveness.

Acknowledgments

This research was funded by the Washington Department of Fish and Wildlife. Transportation of tagged fish from the hatchery to the release site was conducted by Tacoma Power. We are grateful to Mike Blankenship, Teresa Fryer, John Serl, and Wade Heimbigner with the Washington Department of Fish and Wildlife and the Pacific States Marine Fisheries Commission for their contributions during the study. Similarly, Missy Baier, Ross Reichert, and Tony Royce with Tacoma Power provided assistance with fish collection and handling at the Cowlitz Salmon Hatchery. Reviews by Mark Johnson, Bjorn Van-der-leeuw, and Brady Allen greatly improved this report.

References Cited

Berejikian, B.A., Mathews, S.B., and Quinn, T.P., 1996, Effects of hatchery and wild ancestry and rearing environments on the development of agonistic behavior in steelhead trout fry: Canadian Journal of Fisheries and Aquatic Sciences, v. 53, p. 2004–2014.

Hindar, K., Ryman, N., and Utter, F., 1991, Genetic effects of cultured fish on natural populations: Canadian Journal of Fisheries and Aquatic Sciences, v. 48, p. 945–957.

Noakes, D.J., Beamish, R.J., Sweeting, R., and King, J., 2000, Changing the balance—Interactions between hatchery and wild Pacific salmon in the presence of regime shifts: North Pacific Anadromous Fish Commission Bulletin, v. 2, p. 155–163.

Naman, S.W., and Sharpe, C.S., 2012, Predation by hatchery yearling salmonids on wild subyearling salmonids in the freshwater environment A review of studies, two case histories, and implications for management: Environmental Biology of Fishes, v. 94, p. 21–28.

National Marine Fisheries Service, 2011, 5-year review—Summary and evaluation of lower Columbia River Chinook, Columbia River chum, lower Columbia River coho and lower Columbia River steelhead: July 26, 2011, NMFS-NWFSC Status Review Update Memo.

Rand, P.S., Berejikian, B.A., Pearsons, T.N., and Noakes, D.L.G., 2012, Ecological interactions between wild and hatchery salmonids—An introduction to the special issue: Environmental Biology of Fishes, v. 94, p. 1–6.

Waples, R.S., 1991, Dispelling some myths about hatcheries: Fisheries, v. 24, p. 12–21.